College Life

A Gift of Memories

Havoc
PUBLISHING

© 1997 Havoc Publishing

ISBN 1-57977-119-X

Published and created by Havoc Publishing

San Diego, California

First Printing, October 1997

Designed by Juddesign

Made in China

Please write to us for more information on our

Havoc Publishing Record Books and Products.

HAVOC PUBLISHING
9808 Waples Street,
San Diego, CA 92121

College Life

A Gift of Memories for

_____

Contents

Pack It Up, Pack It In

My New Home

About My School

Dorm & Apartment Life

All About My Roommate(s)

Photographs

My Life as a Student

Major & Minors

School Spirit

Get Involved/It's All Greek to Me

New Adjustments

New Emotions

Gettin' Active

Study Study Study

Party All Night Long

Photographs

The Dating Scene

Contents

Hot Spots & Hang Outs

Forget-Me-Nots

Friends O' Mine

That's Entertainment

Photographs

Spring Break!

Campus Times

Surviving Mid-terms

Finals!

Photographs

Road Trips

Adventures & Eye-Opening Experiences

Wild Times

Key Moments

How I Survived

Photographs

Me & My Rosy Summer

Pack It Up, Pack It In

"Everything But The Kitchen Sink" Otherwise known as

Packing-it-all-up stories

I'm gonna miss . . .

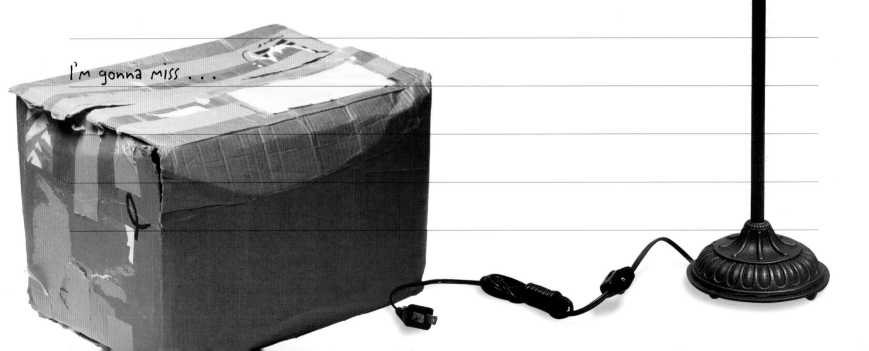

Advice I took with me

Photo

Photo

My New Home!

☐ On campus 👉 address _____

☐ Off campus 👉 address _____

Interesting people I've met so far
_____
_____
_____
_____
_____

Modes of transportation (circle, please)

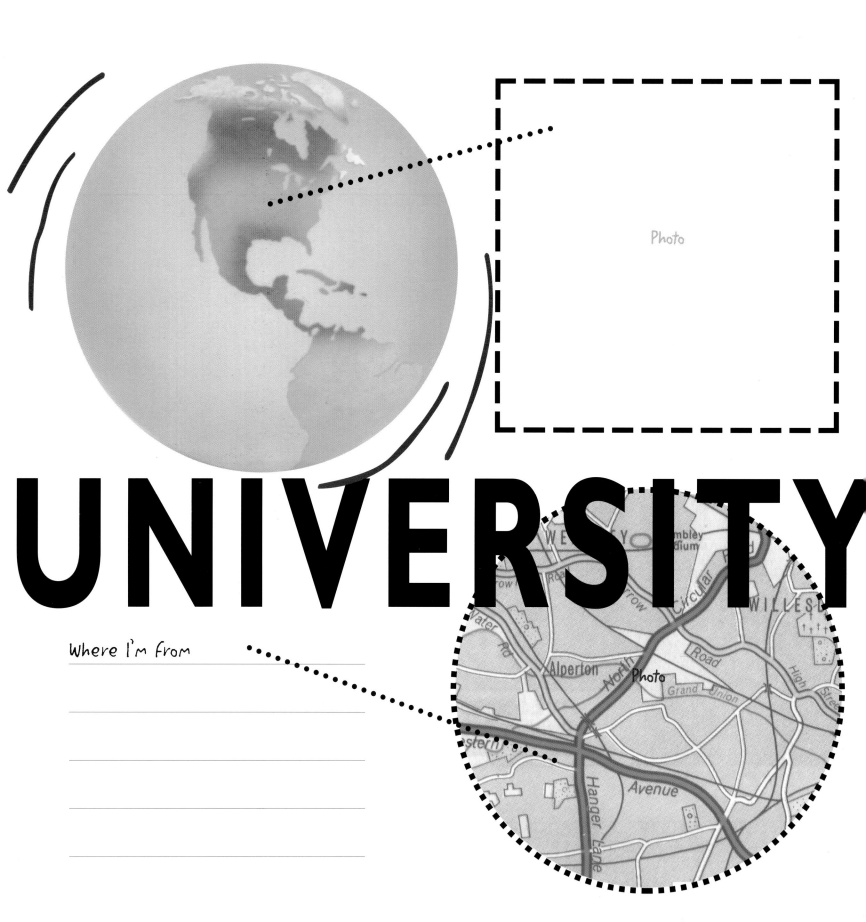

Photo

UNIVERSITY

Where I'm from

Photo

About My SCHOOL

Why I love this school

_____

_____

_____

_____

_____

Best first-week activities

_____

_____

_____

_____

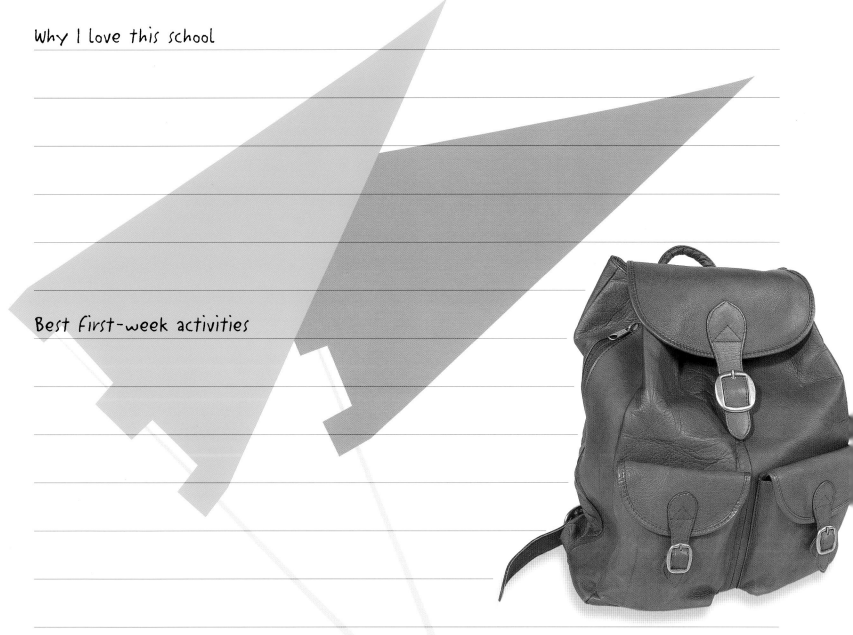

col•lege \kal-ij\ *n*   an independent institution of higher learning . . .

Dorm & Apartment Life

Special memories
_____
_____
_____
_____
_____
_____
_____
_____
_____
_____

About my living space
_____
_____
_____
_____
_____
_____
_____
_____
_____
_____

FALLOUT SHELTER

All About My Roommate(s)

Photograph

Photograph

My Life as a Student

favorite classes

_____

_____

_____

_____

_____

_____

_____

_____

favorite professors

_____

_____

_____

_____

_____

_____

_____

_____

Major & Minors

My major
_____

_____

_____

My minor(s)
_____

_____

How many different majors I've had (descriptions, please)
_____

_____

_____

_____

School Spirit

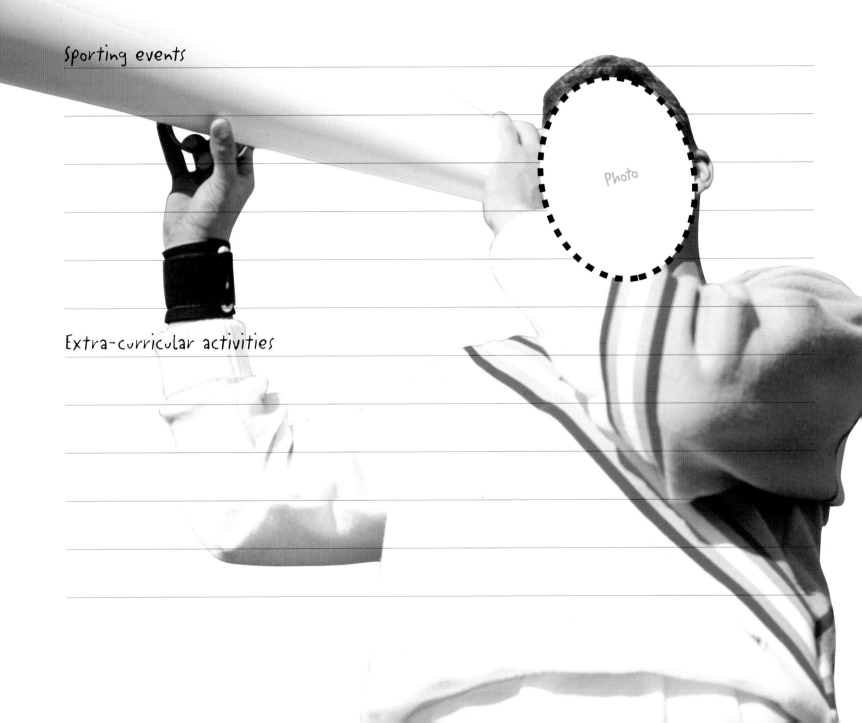

Sporting events

Extra-curricular activities

Photo

Get Involved!

Clubs & organizations

_____

_____

_____

_____

_____

_____

Photo

ΙτΠσ Αλλ Γρεεκ το Με
(It's All Greek to Me)

Memorable stories

_____

_____

_____

_____

_____

_____

_____

_____

_____

_____

_____

_____

_____

_____

New Adjustments

Phone bill stories

Food

The cost of living (i.e. "You mean books cost **that much!?!?**")

New Emotions

I worry about

I'm excited about

Homesickness level:

Cool care packages

From:

□ Unbearable

□ So so

contents:

□ Are you kidding?!

It is best to learn as we go, not go as we have learned — LESLIE JEANNE SAHLER

At every moment, ou bodies are continuall responding to the messages from our mind So what messages is you mind giving your body? - MARGO ADAI

Gettin' Active

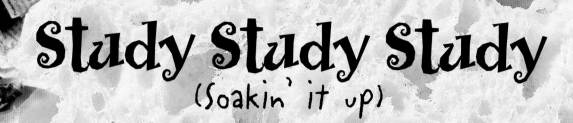

Study Study Study
(Soakin' it up)

Tales of late night studying, all-nighters & cramming

_____

_____

_____

_____

_____

_____

Favorite places to study

_____

_____

_____

Favorite Late-Night Snacks

Never eat more than you can lift - Miss Piggy

Wild parties

Party All

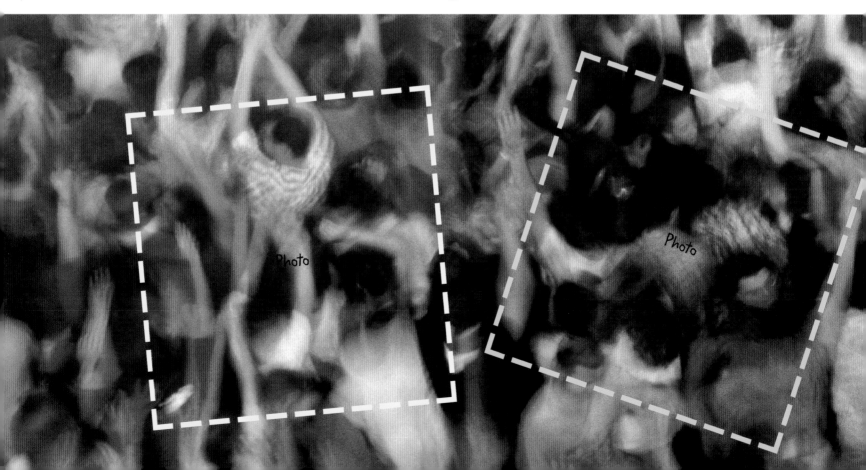

Photo

Photo

I can't believe I did that!

Night Long

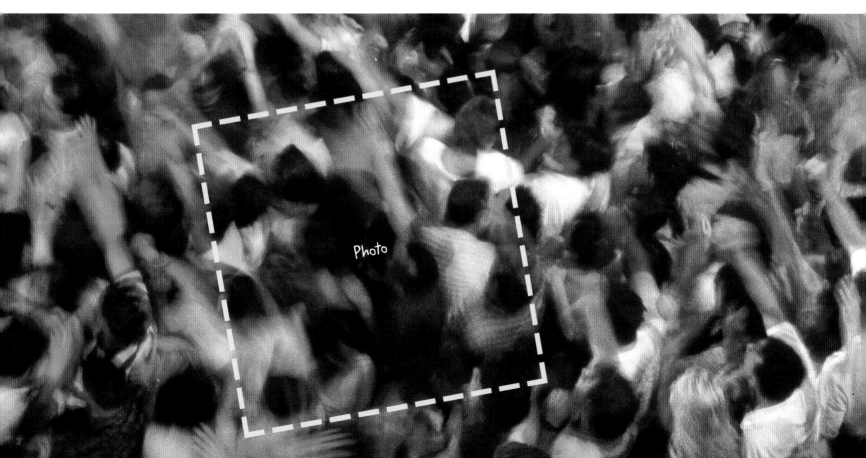

Photo

Photograph

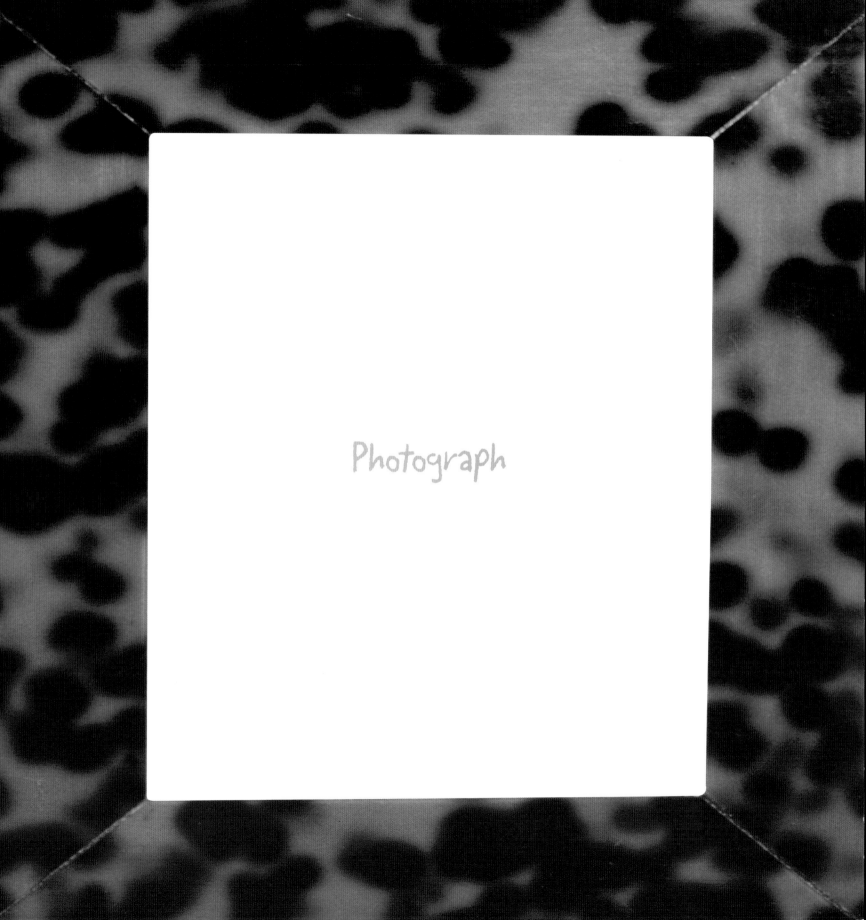

Photograph

The Dating Scene

Meeting new people

Funny stories

The giving of love is an education in itself - **ELEANOR ROOSEVELT**

Hot Spots

Popular bars

Cool clubs

Memorable moments

Hang Outs

Local hangouts

Restaurants

Local hangouts

Favorite java shops

We are the hero of our own story - MARY McCARTHY

Forget-Me-Not's

16

Name

Address

13

Name

Address

15

Name

Address

14

Name

Address

12

Name

Address

Phone Messages

Name

Address

📞

💻

Name

Address

📞

💻

Name

Address

📞

💻

Name

Address

📞

💻

Name

Address

📞

💻

I still hear from

Friends O' Mine

New Friends

Where we go & what we do

Photo

It is the friends you can call up at 4 a.m. that matter - **MARLENE DIETRICH**

That's Entertainment!

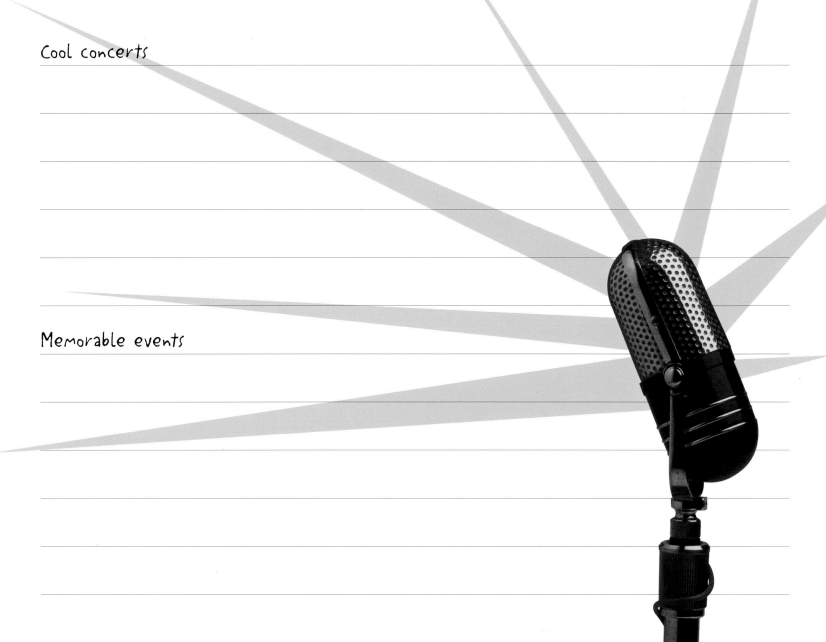

Cool concerts

Memorable events

You were once wild here. Don't let them tame you ISADORA DUNCAN

Photo

Photograph

Photograph

What I did and where I went

Spring Break!

if you obey all the rules you miss all the fun - KATHARINE HEPBURN

CAMPUS TIMES

A DIVISION OF THE HAVOC TIMES

On Campus Highlights

Photo

Photo

Gossip

_____

_____

_____

_____

_____

_____

_____

_____

_____

_____

_____

Photo

What's Happening

_____

_____

_____

_____

_____

_____

Surviving Mid-terms

What I breezed through
_____

_____

_____

What I simply dreaded
_____

_____

_____

_____

How I celebrated after
_____

_____

_____

_____

Photo

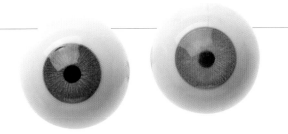

Finals!

What finals I breezed through

What finals I simply dreaded

How I celebrated after

Photograph

Road Trips

Places I traveled

_____

_____

_____

_____

_____

_____

_____

_____

Most adventurous trip

_____

_____

_____

_____

_____

_____

_____

The essence of pleasure is spontaneity - GERMAINE GREER

Destination
1st step:good start

| 0 | 500 | **1000** | 5000 | 10,000 |

favorite places & why

Adventures
& Eye-Opening Experiences

Cerebral experiences

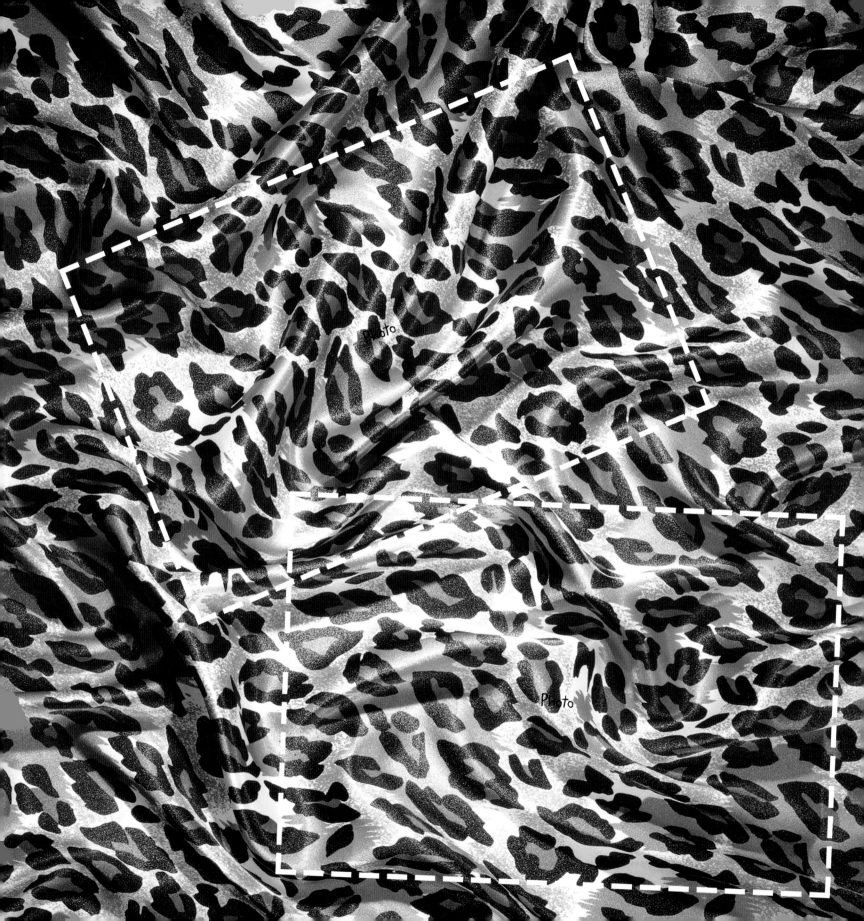

Wild Times

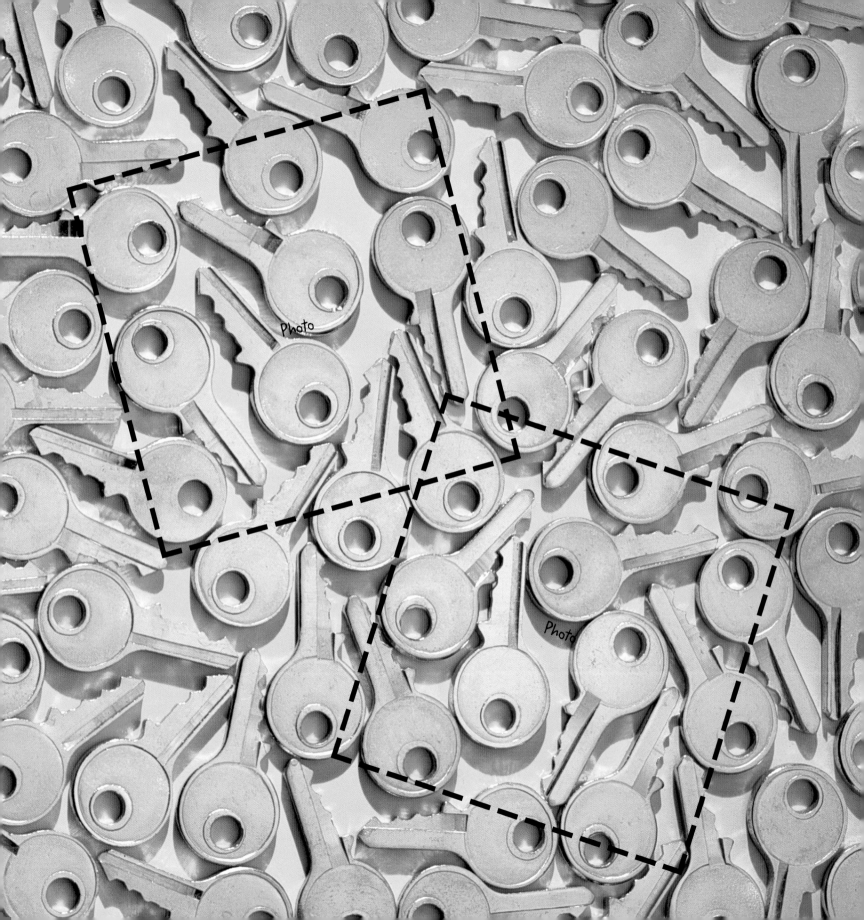

How I Survived

My influences

_____

_____

_____

_____

What I've learned

_____

_____

_____

Things that got me through school

_____

_____

_____

Survival Tips!

Photograph

Photograph

Photo

Me & My Rosy Summer

My checklist

When i look into the future, it's so bright it burns my eyes - OPRAH WINFREY

Available Record Books From Havoc

Baby
Coach
College Life
Couples
Dad
Girlfriends
Golf
Grandmother
Grandparents
Mom

Mothers & Daughters
My Pregnancy
Our Honeymoon
Retirement
School Days
Single Life
Sisters
Teacher
Traveling Adventures
Tying The Knot

Please write to us with your ideas for additional
Havoc Publishing Record Books and Products

HAVOC PUBLISHING
9808 Waples Street,
San Diego. CA 92121